DOLLY

AN UNAUTHORIZED COLLECTION OF

WISE & WITTY WORDS ON GRIT, LIPSTICK, LOVE & LIFE FROM DOLLY PARTON

MARY ZAIA

CASTLE POINT BOOKS
NEW YORK

www.castlepointbooks.com

The Castle Point Books trademark is owned
by Castle Point Publishing, LLC.
Castle Point books are published and distributed by St. Martin's Press.

ISBN 978-1-250-27031-3 (paper over board)
ISBN 978-1-250-27032-0 (ebook)

Cover design by Katie Jennings Campbell
Interior design by Melissa Gerber

Images used under license from Shutterstock.com

Our books may be purchased in bulk for promotional, educational,
or business use. Please contact your local bookseller or the
Macmillan Corporate and Premium Sales Department at 1-800-221-7945,
extension 5442, or by email at MacmillanSpecialMarkets@macmillan.com.

First Edition: April 2020

10 9 8 7 6 5 4 3 2 1

Contents

Hello, Dolly!

WITH HER BIG HAIR, BIG VOICE, AND EVEN BIGGER HEART,
Dolly Parton is Queen of Country, but a diva she is not.
As one of America's most beloved and admired women
for her legendary lyrics, remarkable voice, clever quips,
and empowering truths, she has the power to lift spirits
while keeping her feet firmly on the ground.

From her humble roots as one of 12 children growing
up in the backwoods of the Great Smoky Mountains,
Dolly has risen to become one of the most celebrated
women in the music industry. She may make it look like a
glitzy fairy tale, but her grit, dedication, and unapologetic
spirit are where she truly shines. Dolly wrote her first
song at five years old and is now credited as a songwriter
and composer on thousands more and counting. Her
accomplishments span decades; from her induction
into the Country Music Hall of Fame and eight Grammy

Awards, to multiplatinum albums, 25 Billboard number one hits, Academy Award nominations, and many more, Dolly has earned the most awards and honors of any female country music artist.

Despite all the recognition and razzle-dazzle, she remains genuine and generous, using her success to give back to others. Dolly's strong sense of home led her to invest where her story began in Tennessee. The Dollywood Foundation inspires children in her home community to dream more, learn more, care more, and be more. Dollywood and the Dolly Parton's Stampede dinner theaters have brought new life for visitors and new jobs for residents. Her foundation, Imagination Library, has placed books in the hands of millions of preschool children in need, joining her love of children and devotion to literacy to make a world of difference.

Dolly's charitable efforts, sassy style, and emotive music make her an icon. Yet she's affectionately known as the Dolly-Mama, always ready to lend a listening ear and share her hard-earned secrets on feeling happy, confident, and beautiful even through tough times. It's no wonder the humor in her words and the heart in her songs feel so right. From her own life story to her unforgettable lyrics, Dolly has inspired millions to overcome the odds and rise in strength and love. Let her positive energy and words of **WARMTH, WISDOM, AND WIT** inspire you to live large and love every minute of it.

Brave Enough

YOU'LL NEVER
DO A WHOLE
LOT UNLESS
YOU'RE
brave enough
TO TRY.

"

Living in America
and, of course, just
being women in general,
we've got more

strength

than we think we do.

"

GRIT AND LIPSTICK,
TWO THINGS YOU
SHOULD NEVER LEAVE
HOME WITHOUT.

I have always been
a firm believer in

working hard

for what is right and
for making your own
breaks if you want
things to change.

I THANK GOD
for my failures.
Maybe not at the
time but after
some reflection.
I never feel like a
failure just because
something I tried
has failed.

If you don't like the road you're walking,

START PAVING

another one.

ABOVE THE STORM, THE SMALLEST PRAYER WILL STILL BE HEARD.

THE WAY
I SEE IT, IF
YOU WANT
TO SEE THE
RAINBOW
YOU GOTTA
PUT UP WITH
THE RAIN.

I'VE HAD *heartaches*, HEADACHES, TOOTHACHES, EARACHES, AND I'VE HAD A FEW PAINS IN THE ASS; BUT I'VE *survived* TO TELL ABOUT IT.

STORMS
MAKE
trees
TAKE
DEEPER
roots.

Adjusting to the passage of time,
I think, is a key to success
and to life: just being able to
roll with the punches.

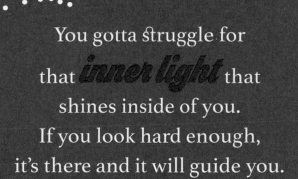

You gotta struggle for
that *inner light* that
shines inside of you.
If you look hard enough,
it's there and it will guide you.

SOMETIMES YOU'VE GOT TO KICK YOUR HEELS OFF and sit down a minute, so you can be ready for your next step!

WE CANNOT DIRECT THE WIND,

but we can adjust the sails.

TUMBLE OUTTA BED
AND I STUMBLE
TO THE KITCHEN
POUR MYSELF A

cup of ambition

—*from "9 to 5"*

SO TRY EACH DAY TO TRY A *little harder* AND IF YOU FALL, GET UP AND *try again*

—*from "Try"*

GOD HAS HIS PLANS
and his reasons.
Sometimes we
are supposed
to go through
things so that we
LEARN LESSONS.

" "

Might be
little,
but I am
loud!

" "

I NEVER TRIED QUITTING, AND I *never quit trying.*

It's hard
to be a

DIAMOND

in a

RHINESTONE

world.

Don't let these

false eyelashes

lead you to believe that I'm
as phony as I look 'cause I run

true and deep.

FIND OUT **WHO YOU ARE.**
AND **DO IT** ON PURPOSE.

I've always kinda
been a little
outcast myself,
a little oddball,
doin' my thing,
my own way.

**IF YOU TRY
TO FOLLOW
EVERYONE ELSE**
and be like everyone
else, before you
know it you're gone.
You're not going to
find yourself again;
you'll just be a
version of what
you might have
hoped to have been.

We're all just
a bunch of
sinners, but
**WE DO THE
BEST WE CAN.**

No one is ever
successful at
everything
that they do.

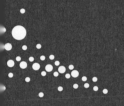

We need to be

accepting

of ourselves

in how we are.

HE'S ALWAYS LOVED WHO I WAS, AND I LOVED WHO HE WAS, AND WE NEVER TRIED TO CHANGE EACH OTHER.

—*on her marriage to Carl Dean*

I DON'T CARE
WHO PEOPLE
ARE AS LONG
AS THEY'RE
THEMSELVES,
WHATEVER
THAT IS.

EVERYONE SHOULD BE WITH WHO THEY *love.*

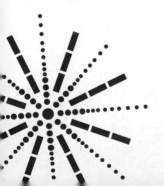

I AM NOT GAY,
BUT IF I WERE,
I WOULD BE
the first
ONE RUNNING OUT
OF THE CLOSET.

I'M PROUD OF MY
HILLBILLY, WHITE TRASH
BACKGROUND. TO ME THAT
keeps you humble;
THAT KEEPS YOU GOOD.
AND IT DOESN'T MATTER HOW
HARD YOU TRY TO OUTRUN
IT—IF THAT'S WHO YOU ARE,
that's who you are.

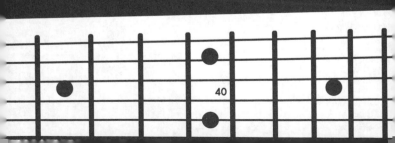

I DON'T LIKE TO
GIVE ADVICE.
I LIKE TO GIVE
PEOPLE INFORMATION,
BECAUSE EVERYONE'S
life is different,
AND EVERYONE'S
journey is different.

I KNOW WHO I AM, I know what I can and can't do. I know what I will and won't do.

I KNOW WHAT I'M CAPABLE OF and I don't agree to do things that I don't think I can pull off.

I still close my eyes
and go home—
I CAN ALWAYS
DRAW FROM THAT.

I'm comfortable in

MY OWN SKIN,

no matter how
far it's stretched.

66

I never have changed
in my taste, and the things
that I love, and the way
that I act, and all that.
I never wanted to change,
I just wanted to be successful,
and be able to do more
things for more people,
and for myself as well.

99

It's you
WHO SETS
YOUR STRIDE!

I HOPE LIFE TREATS YOU KIND
AND I HOPE YOU'LL HAVE ALL
THAT YOU EVER DREAMED OF

I wish you joy

AND I WISH YOU HAPPINESS

BUT ABOVE ALL THIS

I wish you love

—*from "I Will Always Love You"*

I ALWAYS ASK
GOD TO WORK
THROUGH ME AND
let me be a light
OF SOME KIND AND
HELP IN THIS WORLD.

FUNNY THING IS
THAT THE POORER
PEOPLE ARE, THE
more generous
THEY SEEM TO BE.

You can be

rich in spirit,

kindness, love, and all
those things that you
can't put a dollar sign on.

WE SHOULD **ALWAYS** BE READY TO LEND A HAND WHEN SOMEONE IS HURTING.

I have a strict policy that
nobody cries alone
in my presence.

I'LL NEVER HARDEN

my heart, but I've
toughened the
muscles around it.

Love is like
A BUTTERFLY,
a rare and
gentle thing

—*from "Love Is Like a Butterfly"*

NO MATTER WHAT, I ALWAYS MAKE IT HOME FOR CHRISTMAS.

TELL ME I HAVE TO
BE SOMEWHERE,
AND I'LL BE THERE
20 MINUTES EARLY
AND STAY THERE
LONGER THAN
ANYBODY
ELSE.

I just feel God didn't mean
for me to have kids so that
everybody else's children
could be mine.

I believe

that every child
Needs to feel a sense
of pride and
Someone to love
and guide, and
see them through

—*from "Red Shoes"*

THERE'S A PLACE
for all of us
IF WE'D REACH OUT
AND TOUCH THE LOVE
NOTHING'S GONNA
EVER CHANGE IT
MUCH IF WE DON'T

—from "If We Don't"

As Good as I Can

WHEN I WAKE UP, I EXPECT THINGS TO BE GOOD.

If they're not, then I try to set about trying to make them as good as I can, 'cause I know I'm gonna have to live that day anyway.

Some people
work at being
MISERABLE.
I work at being
HAPPY.

When folks ask
for my advice on

STAYING POSITIVE,

I just tell 'em it's
simple! All the healing
starts with you.

If you're feeling low,
don't despair.
The sun has a sinking
spell every night,
but it comes back up
every morning.

THEY THINK I'M
SIMPLEMINDED BECAUSE
I SEEM TO BE HAPPY.
*Why shouldn't
I be happy?*
I HAVE EVERYTHING
I EVER WANTED AND
MORE. MAYBE I AM
SIMPLEMINDED. MAYBE
THAT'S THE KEY: SIMPLE.

66

Wouldn't it be something
if we could have

things we love

in abundance without their
losing that special
attraction the want of
them held for us.

99

I'M A GYPSY

at heart.

I JUST LOVE
THE ROCKING
OF THOSE
WHEELS AND
SMELL OF DIESEL.

I'M NOT HAPPY ALL THE
TIME, AND I WOULDN'T
WANT TO BE BECAUSE
THAT WOULD MAKE ME
A SHALLOW PERSON.
BUT I DO TRY TO
find the good
IN EVERYBODY.

LIFE IS SWEETER WHEN YOU HAVE AN ATTITUDE OF GRATITUDE!

One is only poor
Only if they
choose to be

—*from "Coat of Many Colors"*

I MAKE A POINT TO APPRECIATE *all the little things* IN MY LIFE. I GO OUT AND SMELL THE AIR AFTER A GOOD, HARD RAIN. I REREAD PASSAGES FROM MY FAVORITE BOOKS. I HOLD THE LITTLE TREASURES THAT SOMEBODY SPECIAL GAVE ME. THESE SMALL ACTIONS HELP REMIND ME THAT THERE ARE SO MANY GREAT, GLORIOUS PIECES OF GOOD IN THE WORLD.

"

When I meet someone,
I look at their eyes and
their smile and seek out the

good first.

"

GROWING UP IN THE MOUNTAINS OF EAST TENNESSEE, WE GOT SO MUCH OF WHAT WE NEEDED FROM THE LAND. I'LL ALWAYS BE GRATEFUL TO THE LAND AND TO NATURE FOR ALL IT'S GIVEN US!

MY RELATIONSHIPS
WITH MY FAMILY,
MY MUSIC,
AND MY GOD
HAVE ALWAYS
BEEN THE MOST
IMPORTANT
THINGS THAT
HAVE KEPT ME
CENTERED AND
GROUNDED.

75

Don't get so busy
making a living that
you forget to

MAKE A LIFE.

Leave

SOMETHING GOOD

in every day.

If you see someone without a smile today,

GIVE 'EM YOURS!

Straight Talk

GIMME SOME STRAIGHT TALK, *straight talk* AND HOLD THE SUGAR PLEASE

—from "Straight Talk"

WHEN I GOT SOMETHIN' TO SAY,

I'll say it.

If there's a heaven,

I hope to hell I go!

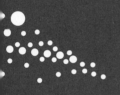

I was the first woman to

burn my bra—

it took the fire department
four days to put it out.

PEOPLE SAY,
"OH, YOU JUST
ALWAYS SEEM
SO HAPPY."
*Well, that's
the Botox.*

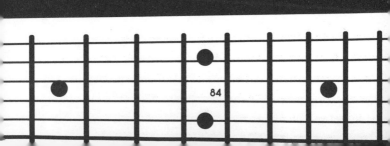

84

THE SECRET
TO A LONG
MARRIAGE
IS TO
stay gone.

I'M NOT
INTIMIDATED
by how people
perceive me.

I walk *tall;* I got a tall *attitude.*

I JUST
DON'T
FEEL
LIKE I
HAVE TO
explain
MYSELF.

I'm not offended
by all the dumb

blonde jokes

because I know I'm not
dumb...and I also
know that
I'm not blonde.

A positive attitude
and a sense of humor
go together like
biscuits and gravy.

Show business IS A MONEY-
MAKING JOKE.
AND I'VE JUST
ALWAYS LIKED
TELLING JOKES!

"

I've been told a few
times I should run for

president,

but I think there are enough
boobs in the race already.

"

MY WEAKNESSES
have always been
FOOD AND MEN—
in that order.

My **FAVORITE DISH** is anything that starts and ends with a potato!

WHEN SOMEONE
SHOWS YOU THEIR
TRUE COLORS,
BELIEVE THEM.

I'M OLD
ENOUGH
AND
CRANKY
ENOUGH
NOW THAT
IF SOMEONE
TRIED TO TELL
ME WHAT TO
DO, I'D TELL
THEM WHERE
TO PUT IT.

I don't
kiss
nobody's
butt.

I've got
everything
I need...
Jesus
and
gravity.

Mama always said

I HAD A WAY WITH WORDS.

DREAMS are
of no value
if they're not
equipped
with **WINGS.**

I just kind of
wake up with
a new idea
and new dreams
every day, and
I FOLLOW
THAT DREAM.

MY FIRST SONG WAS ABOUT
MY CORNCOB DOLL, BUT I
WAS SO LITTLE MY MAMA
HAD TO WRITE THE LYRICS
DOWN. EVEN THEN,

I had big dreams!

SOME OF MY
dreams
ARE SO
BIG, THEY'D
SCARE YOU.

I WON'T
LIMIT MYSELF

just because people
won't accept I can do
something else.

Sometimes, you see folks who have a negative view of dreamers—people who sit around all day on their hindquarters and do absolutely nothing. These folks aren't dreamers—they are just lazy. To me,

dreaming is just part of being alive,

inspired, and curious about the world.

WHEN I'M
INSPIRED,
I get excited
BECAUSE I CAN'T
WAIT TO SEE
WHAT I'LL COME
UP WITH NEXT.

66

I look like a woman but

I think like a man.

And in this world of business, that
has helped me a lot. Because by
the time they think that I don't
know what's goin' on, I then got
the money, and am gone.

99

I CAN'T DO NOTHING
JUST A LITTLE.

I really wish that y'all
could have seen the
look on my lawyer's
face when I told him
I wanted to start a
theme park and call it
Dollywood.

I think that all
CREATIVE PEOPLE
are a little bit nuts.

I REFUSE TO SETTLE

for something less than great. And if it takes a lifetime, then that's how long I'll wait. Is that too much to ask?

THE MAGIC IS INSIDE YOU. THERE AIN'T NO CRYSTAL BALL!

IT'S OKAY
TO CHANGE
DREAMS

IN THE
MIDDLE
OF THE
STREAM.

IT'S IMPORTANT
THAT KIDS HAVE
SOMEONE WHO
encourages
THEM TO CHASE
THEIR RAINBOW.

66

I believe that if every
kid grows up with a song
in their heart and a book
in their hand, there's a pretty
good chance that their

*dreams will
come true!*

99

IF YOUR ACTIONS CREATE A LEGACY THAT INSPIRES OTHERS *to dream more, learn more, do more* **AND BECOME MORE, THEN, YOU ARE AN EXCELLENT LEADER.**

No
Rhinestone
Unturned

I never let a

rhinestone

go unturned!

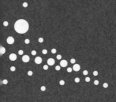

I just always wanted to be
shiny and *sparkly*.

MY SMILE'S PRETTY HARD TO MISS, considering I'm a gal who likes her lipstick—the redder, the better.

I FEEL GLAMOROUS ON THE INSIDE,

so I want to look like it on the outside.

WHEN I'M FEELING

a little low,

I PUT ON MY FAVORITE
HIGH HEELS TO STAND

a little taller.

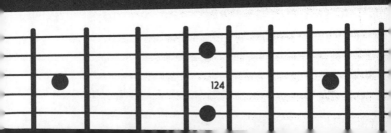

I WOULD NEVER STOOP SO LOW AS TO BE *fashionable.*

I dress to be
comfortable
FOR ME.

" Every *sequin* tells a *story.* "

IT'S A GOOD
THING I WAS
BORN A GIRL,
OTHERWISE
I'D BE A
drag queen.

People always ask me how long it takes to do my hair. I don't know,

I'm never there.

IF ANYONE TELLS YOU
YOUR HAIR IS TOO BIG,
GET RID OF THEM. YOU
DON'T NEED THAT KIND OF
NEGATIVITY IN YOUR LIFE.

THE BIGGER THE HAIR, THE CLOSER TO GOD.

I tried every diet in the book.

I TRIED SOME THAT WEREN'T IN THE BOOK. I TRIED EATING THE BOOK. IT TASTED BETTER THAN MOST OF THE DIETS.

My fat never made me
less money.

IF I CAN GET MY DRESS ON,
MY WEIGHT IS UNDER CONTROL.

The only way I'd be caught without makeup

is if my radio fell in the bathtub
while I was taking a bath and
electrocuted me and I was
in between makeup at home.
I hope my husband would slap
a little lipstick on me before he
took me to the morgue.

IT COSTS
A LOT OF
MONEY
TO LOOK
THIS
CHEAP!

Life Is a Song

Life is

a song to me

My songs are the

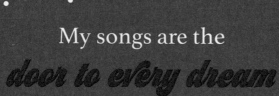

I've ever had and every
success I've ever achieved.

My nails are my rhythm section

WHEN I'M WRITING A SONG ALL ALONE. SOMEDAY, I MAY CUT AN ALBUM, JUST ME AND MY NAILS.

I GOT THE MUSIC
IN MY SOUL AND
THE RHYTHM IN
MY FEET. WHEN I
hear the music,
YOU WON'T CATCH
ME STANDING STILL.

SONGWRITING is my way of **CHANNELING MY FEELINGS** and my thoughts. Not just mine, but the things I see, the people I care about. My head would explode if I didn't get some of that stuff out.

IF YOU TALK BAD ABOUT COUNTRY MUSIC, it's like saying bad things about my momma. **THEM'S FIGHTIN' WORDS.**

I LOVE STORY
SONGS BECAUSE
*I've always
loved books.*

"

Some days you'll
get one song, and some
days you'll get five. And the
moral to that story is, all
that matters is you
keep doing it.

"

I'VE HAD

more guts

THAN I'VE GOT

talent.

146

Being a star
JUST MEANS
THAT YOU JUST
FIND YOUR OWN
SPECIAL PLACE,
AND THAT YOU
SHINE WHERE
YOU ARE.

I've always
worked more for
THE REWARDS
than the awards.
I've always counted
MY BLESSINGS
before I've
counted my money.

Still the Same Girl

I'M STILL THE *same girl* THAT WANTS TO SQUEEZE EVERY LITTLE DROP OUT OF LIFE THAT I CAN.

In my mind, I'll be 35

forever.

Stop this attitude THAT OLDER PEOPLE AIN'T ANY GOOD ANYMORE! WE'RE AS GOOD AS WE EVER WERE— IF WE EVER WERE ANY GOOD.

I SAY THAT
I'M AS OLD
AS YESTERDAY,
BUT HOPEFULLY
as new as
tomorrow.

I don't know what the big deal is about old age. Old people who **SHINE FROM THE INSIDE** look 10 to 20 years younger.

I WON'T MISS A BEAT.

I never have,
I never will.

I JUST DON'T HAVE
TIME TO **GET OLD!**

The older I get, the earlier
I get up. The second my feet
hit the floor, I'm awake. I'm
like hurry, hurry.

I just love life.

And I feel like we ain't got
but a certain amount of
time anyway. I want to make
the most of all of it.

WHEN I SIT BACK
IN MY ROCKER,
I WANT TO HAVE
done it all.

I want to go and go, and then drop dead in the middle of something I'm loving to do. And if that doesn't happen, if I wind up sitting in a wheelchair, at least I'll have my

high heels on.

IF I'M REMEMBERED 100 YEARS FROM NOW, I HOPE IT WILL BE NOT FOR LOOKS BUT FOR BOOKS.